The Usborne

Very First
Dictionary
in French

Felicity Brooks, Caroline Young and Claire Masset
Designed by Francesca Allen and Keith Newell
Illustrated by Jo Litchfield

Contents

Here are some children you will meet in this book.

Ellie

Ben

Molly

Polly Jack

Robert

Laura

Olly Emily

You can hear all the French words in this book, read by a French person, on the Usborne Quicklinks Website at **www.usborne-quicklinks.com** Find out more on page 80.

Aa

afternoon

l'après-midi (m)

a sunny **afternoon**
un **après-midi** ensoleillé

all   **tout** (m), **toute** (f),
tous, toutes

They are **all** playing music.
Ils jouent **tous** de la musique.

about   **sur**

He reads a book **about** school.

Il lit un livre **sur** l'école.

again   **encore**

The little girl   La petite fille
bounces, and   bondit, et
bounces **again**.   bondit **encore**.

alphabet

l'alphabet (m)

abcdefgh
ijklmnopq
rstuvwxyz

after   **après**

one after
the other

l'une **après**
l'autre

air   **l'air** (m), **les airs**

Balloons   Les
float in   montgolfières
the **air**.   volent dans
               les **airs**.

always   **toujours**

Tom **always**   Tom met
wears socks.   **toujours** des
                   chaussettes.

ambulance　l'ambulance (f)

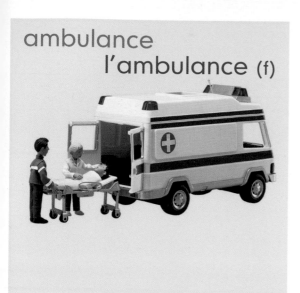

animal　l'animal (m), les animaux

some farm animals　　des animaux de la ferme

ant　la fourmi

some ants　　des fourmis

angel　l'ange (m)

ankle　la cheville

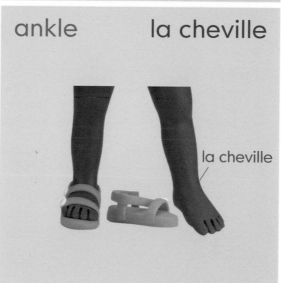

la cheville

any　du (m), de la (f), des (plural)

Is there any soup?

Est-ce qu'il y a de la soupe ?

angry　fâché

This girl looks angry.

Cette fille a l'air fâché.

another　encore

Danny wants another lemonade.　Danny veut encore une limonade.

apple　la pomme

are — sont

The monkeys **are** brown.

Les singes **sont** marron.

asleep — endormi

Shhh! The little boy's **asleep**.

Chut ! Le petit garçon est **endormi**.

Bb

arm — le bras

le bras

astronaut — l'astronaute (m/f)

baby — le bébé

ask — demander

The girl **asks** who's on the phone.

La fille **demande** qui est à l'appareil.

awake — éveillé, réveillé

They are still **awake**.

Ils sont encore **éveillés**.

bad — mauvais

The apple tastes **bad**.

La pomme a **mauvais** goût.

bag — le sac

banana — la banane

beach — la plage

ball — le ballon, la balle

basket — le panier

bear — l'ours (m)

balloon — le ballon

three **balloons**   trois **ballons**

bath — le bain

She is having a bath.   Elle prend un bain.

bed — le lit

bee   l'abeille (f)

big   grand

Swans are **big** birds.

Les cygnes sont de **grands** oiseaux.

bite   la bouchée

The boy is taking a bite.

Le garçon prend une bouchée.

belt   la ceinture

bird   l'oiseau (m), les oiseaux

blanket   la couverture

bicycle   la bicyclette, le vélo

birthday   l'anniversaire (m)

a **birthday** cake

un gâteau d'anniversaire

boat   le bateau, les bateaux

bone — l'os (m), les os

This x-ray shows the boy's bones.

Cette radio montre les os du garçon.

bowl — le bol

The bowl is full.

Le bol est plein.

bread — le pain

book — le livre

box — la boîte

breakfast — le petit déjeuner

boots — les bottes (f)

boy — le garçon

brother — le frère

two brothers — deux frères

brush   la brosse

butterfly   le papillon

Cc

build   construire

The men **build** a wall.

Les hommes **construisent** un mur.

button   le bouton

some **buttons**   des **boutons**

cake   le gâteau,
les gâteaux

bus   l'autobus (m),
le bus

buy   acheter

He is buying
a lollipop.

Il **achète** une sucette.

can   pouvoir

How many girls **can** you see?

Tu **peux** voir combien de filles ?

car   la voiture

cat   le chat

cheese   le fromage

carrot   la carotte

two carrots   deux carottes

catch   attraper

"Catch!" says the boy.

"Attrape !" dit le garçon.

cherry   la cerise

red cherries   des cerises rouges

castle   le château, les châteaux

chair   la chaise

chicken   le poulet

two chickens   deux poulets

chocolate **le chocolat**

cloud **le nuage**

come **venir**

The clown **comes** to Luke's house.

Le clown **vient** chez Luke.

clock **la pendule**

coat **le manteau,**
les manteaux

computer **l'ordinateur** (m)

clothes **les vêtements** (m)

warm **clothes**

des **vêtements** chauds

cold **froid**

It's **cold** in winter.

Il fait **froid** en hiver.

cook **faire la cuisine**

Sam **cooks.** Sam **fait la cuisine.**

cow   la vache

Dd

day   le jour

The sun rises every day.

Le soleil se lève tous les jours.

cry   pleurer

The little boy is crying.
Le petit garçon pleure.

dance   danser

This girl loves to dance.

Cette fille aime danser.

deep   profond

Diggers make deep holes.

Les pelleteuses font des trous profonds.

cup   la tasse

dark   noir

It's dark outside.

Il fait noir dehors.

dentist   le/la dentiste

dig   creuser

Anna is digging a hole.

Anna creuse un trou.

dirty   sale

The digger is dirty.

La pelleteuse est **sale**.

dog   le chien

digger   la pelleteuse

do   faire

There's lots to **do** at the beach.

Il y a beaucoup à **faire** à la plage.

doll   la poupée

dinosaur   le dinosaure

doctor   le médecin, le docteur

donkey   l'âne (m)

door   la porte

dress   la robe

drum   le tambour

This boy is playing a drum.

Ce garçon joue du tambour.

dragon   le dragon

drink   la boisson

a cold drink   une boisson fraîche

dry   sec (m), sèche (f)

The washing is dry.

Le linge est sec.

draw   dessiner

This girl likes drawing.

Cette fille aime dessiner.

drive   conduire

This woman drives a red car.

Cette femme conduit une voiture rouge.

duck   le canard

Ee

ear   l'oreille (f)

egg   l'œuf (m)

three **eggs**   trois **œufs**

each   chaque

Each child has a toy.   Chaque enfant a un jouet.

Earth   la Terre

elbow   le coude

le coude

eagle   l'aigle (m)

eat   manger

This boy is eating pasta.   Ce garçon mange des pâtes.

elephant   l'éléphant (m)

empty — vide

The bath is **empty**.

La baignoire est **vide**.

Ff

family — la famille

end — le bout

There's a girl at each **end**.

Il y a une fille à chaque **bout**.

face — le visage

a happy face — un **visage** souriant

farm — la ferme

eye — l'œil (m), les yeux

fairy — la fée

fast — vite

This car goes very **fast**.

Cette voiture va très **vite**.

fat gros (m), grosse (f)

This cat is fat.

Ce chat est gros.

fire engine la voiture de pompiers

flag le drapeau, les drapeaux

finger le doigt

le doigt

firefighter le pompier

floor le sol

The floor is clean.

Le sol est propre.

fire le feu

fish le poisson

lots of fish beaucoup de poissons

flower la fleur

fly — voler

These birds are flying.

Ces oiseaux volent.

forest — la forêt

friend — l'ami (m), l'amie (f)

food — la nourriture

fork — la fourchette

frog — la grenouille

foot — le pied

le pied

fox — le renard

fruit — les fruits (m)

Gg

gate   **la barrière**

giraffe   **la girafe**

two **giraffes**   deux **girafes**

game   **le jeu,**
les jeux

ghost   **le fantôme**

girl   **la fille**

three **girls**   trois **filles**

garden   **le jardin**

giant   **le géant**

give   **donner**

She **gives** her friend a present.

Elle **donne** un cadeau à son amie.

glass — le verre

These **glasses** are empty.

Ces **verres** sont vides.

go — aller

This bus **goes** to the supermarket.

Ce bus **va** au supermarché.

goldfish — le poisson rouge

glasses — les lunettes (f)

goat — la chèvre

two **goats**

deux **chèvres**

good — bon (m), bonne (f)

These cakes look **good**.

Ces gâteaux ont l'air **bon**.

gloves — les gants (m)

gold — l'or (m)

goose — l'oie (f)

grapes   **le raisin**

grow   **pousser**

These flowers **grow** quickly.

Ces fleurs **poussent** vite.

Hh

grass   **l'herbe** (f), **la pelouse**

grown-up   **la grande personne**

a boy and a **grown-up**

un garçon et une **grande personne**

hair   **les cheveux** (m)

les cheveux

ground   **la terre**

The girl falls on the **ground**.

La fille tombe par **terre**.

guinea pig   **le cochon d'Inde**

hamster   **le hamster**

hand la main	hat le chapeau, les chapeaux	helicopter l'hélicoptère (m)

la main

happy heureux (m), heureuse (f)

head la tête

help aider

The boy **helps** his dad with the shopping. Le garçon **aide** son papa à faire les courses.

hard dur

Stones are very **hard**.

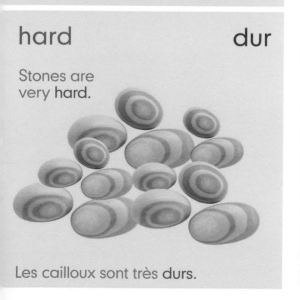

Les cailloux sont très **durs**.

hear entendre

Jack **hears** a noise. Jack **entend** un bruit.

hide se cacher

The clown is hiding.

Le clown se cache.

hit — frapper

Lucy **hits** the ball.

Lucy **frappe** la balle.

honey — le miel

horse — le cheval, les chevaux

hole — le trou

This cheese has **holes** in it.

Ce fromage a des **trous**.

hood — la capuche

hospital — l'hôpital (m), les hôpitaux

home — la maison

hop — sauter à cloche-pied

Can you hop?

Tu sais sauter à cloche-pied ?

hot — chaud

The pans are **hot**.

Les casseroles sont **chaudes**.

house   la maison

I i

idea   l'idée (f)

John has
an idea.

John a
une idée.

h
i

hug   embrasser

Olly hugs his
teddy bear.

Olly embrasse
son nounours.

ice   la glace

some ice   de la glace

if   si

If you go out, take your umbrella.

Si tu sors, prends ton parapluie.

hurt   faire mal

Mark's arm hurts.

Le bras de Mark lui fait mal.

ice cream   la glace

ink   l'encre (f)

green ink

de l'encre verte

insect   l'insecte (m)

some insects   des insectes

is   est

The soup
is delicious.

La soupe
est délicieuse.

Jj

invitation
l'invitation (f)

Olivia invite
Francesca
à son anniversaire
le 13 février à 3 heures.

island   l'île (f)

jacket   la veste

iron   le fer à repasser

itch   démanger

Fred's ear
itches.

L'oreille de Fred
le démange.

jar   le pot

two jars
of jam

deux pots
de confiture

jeans — **le jean, les jeans**

jigsaw puzzle — **le puzzle**

juice — **le jus**

jewel — **la pierre précieuse**

There are jewels in the crown. — Il y a des **pierres précieuses** sur la couronne.

job — **l'emploi** (m)

Vicky has a **job** as a vet. — Vicky a un **emploi** de vétérinaire.

jump — **sauter**

One cat **jumps** off the sofa.

Un chat **saute** du canapé.

jewellery **les bijoux** (m)

juggle — **jongler**

The clown can **juggle**. — Le clown sait **jongler**.

jungle — **la jungle**

Kk

key   **la clé, la clef**

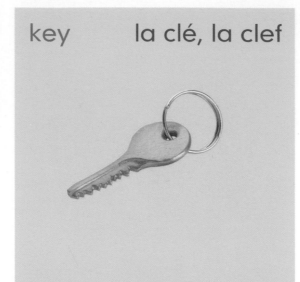

kiss   **le baiser**

His mum gives him a kiss.

Sa maman lui donne un **baiser**.

kangaroo   **le kangourou**

kick   **donner un coup de pied**

He kicks the ball.

Il donne un coup de pied dans le ballon.

kitchen   **la cuisine**

ketchup   **le ketchup**

king   **le roi**

kite   **le cerf-volant**

kitten   le chaton

five kittens   cinq chatons

Ll

lamp   la lampe

knee   le genou,
les genoux

— le genou

ladybird   la coccinelle

laugh   rire

These children are laughing.   Ces enfants rient.

knife   le couteau,
les couteaux

lamb   l'agneau (m),
les agneaux

leaf   la feuille

green leaves

des feuilles vertes

k
l

27

leg — la jambe

la jambe

letter — la lettre

This is the **letter** C.

Voici la **lettre** C.

like — aimer

Cats **like** to play.

Les chats aiment jouer.

lemon — le citron

three lemons

trois citrons

lie — être couché

Kirsty is lying in bed.

Kirsty **est couchée** dans le lit.

lion — le lion

let — laisser

Eve **lets** Bob play with her scooter.

Eve **laisse** Bob jouer avec sa trottinette.

light — clair

It's **light** during the day.

Il fait **clair** dans la journée.

lips — les lèvres (f)

la lèvre

L

listen   écouter

Jack is listening.

Jack écoute.

long   long (m), longue (f)

Amy has long hair.

Amy a les cheveux longs.

loud   fort

WOOF, WOOF!

WOUAH, WOUAH !

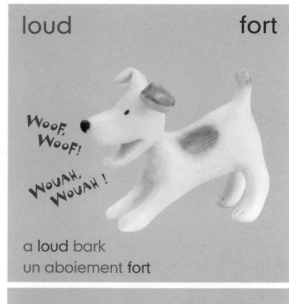

a loud bark
un aboiement fort

little   petit

He's little.

Il est petit.

look (at)   regarder

They are looking at the picture.

Ils regardent l'image.

love   aimer

The children love painting.

Les enfants aiment faire de la peinture.

live   habiter

A family lives here.

Une famille habite ici.

lots   beaucoup

Spot has lots of puppies.

Spot a beaucoup de chiots.

lunch   le déjeuner

l

Mm

make — **faire**

They are making cakes. — Ils font des gâteaux.

mermaid — **la sirène**

machine — **la machine**

a sewing machine — une machine à coudre

man — **l'homme** (m)

mess — **le désordre**

magic — **la magie**

map — **la carte**

milk — **le lait**

mirror la glace, le miroir

monster le monstre

morning le matin

a beautiful morning un beau matin

money l'argent (m)

moon la lune

motorbike la moto

He's riding a motorbike. Il fait de la moto.

m

monkey le singe

more plus

Which arm has more birds on it?

Sur quel bras y a-t-il plus d'oiseaux ?

mountain la montagne

mouse   **la souris**

mud   **la boue**

This girl has **mud** on her.

Cette fille a de la **boue** sur elle.

Nn

mouth   **la bouche**

la bouche

mushroom   **le champignon**

name   **le nom**

Olivia

move   **déplacer**

Tom and Ian **move** the parcel.

Tom et Ian **déplacent** le paquet.

music   **la musique**

naughty   **vilain**

This dog is **naughty**.

Ce chien est **vilain**.

M
N

32

near — près

The tractor is near the wall. / Le tracteur est près du mur.

need — avoir besoin

Sam needs boots today.

Sam a besoin de bottes aujourd'hui.

nest — le nid

a bird's nest / un nid d'oiseaux

neck — le cou

le cou

needle — l'aiguille (f)

net — le filet

a fishing net

un filet de pêche

necklace — le collier

neighbour — le voisin

They are neighbours. / Ils sont voisins.

never — jamais

Never play with matches.

Ne joue jamais avec les allumettes.

m
n

new   **neuf** (m), **neuve** (f)

a **new** bag   un sac **neuf**

nobody   **personne**

Nobody lives here.
Personne n'habite ici.

not   **ne...pas**

He is **not** feeling well.

Il **ne** se sent **pas** bien.

newspaper   **le journal**

noise   **le bruit**

Babies make a lot of **noise**.   Les bébés font beaucoup de **bruit**.

Waa!
Waa!

Ouin !
Ouin !

nothing   **rien**

There's **nothing** in the box.   Il n'y a **rien** dans la boîte.

night   **la nuit**

a starry **night**   une **nuit** étoilée

nose   **le nez**

le nez —

now   **maintenant**

There are four children **now**.
Il y a quatre enfants **maintenant**.

number — le chiffre, le numéro, le nombre

5

This is the number five.
Voici le chiffre cinq.

Oo

of — de

a piece of cake

un morceau de gâteau

nurse — l'infirmier (m), l'infirmière (f)

o'clock — heure (f), heures

three o'clock in the afternoon — trois heures de l'après-midi

often — souvent

She often takes Spot for a walk.

Elle promène souvent Spot.

nut*

a walnut
une noix

some hazelnuts
des noisettes

some peanuts
des cacahuètes

octopus — la pieuvre

oil — l'huile (f)

* In French, there is no word for **nut**. There are only words for different kinds of nuts.

old — vieux (m), vieil (m), vieille (f)

an old woman and an old man
une vieille femme et un vieil homme

only — seulement

The orange cat has only one cushion.

Le chat orange a seulement un coussin.

orange — l'orange (f)

once — une fois

He takes a shower once a day.

Il prend une douche une fois par jour.

open — ouvrir

Alice opens the door.

Alice ouvre la porte.

other — l'autre (m/f)

Where is the other sock?

Où est l'autre chaussette ?

onion — l'oignon (m)

or — ou

Do you want pasta or soup?

Vous voulez des pâtes ou de la soupe ?

owl — le hibou

O
P

Pp

palace — le palais

park — le parc

page — la page

She's turning the page.

Elle tourne la page.

panda — le panda

party — la fête

paint — peindre

She is painting.

Elle peint.

paper — le papier

He's folding some paper.

Il plie du papier.

pasta — les pâtes (f)

o
p

peach la pêche	**pen** le stylo	**people** les gens (m/f)

peach   la pêche

pen   le stylo

three pens   trois stylos

people   les gens (m/f)

There are lots of **people** at the market.   Il y a beaucoup de **gens** au marché.

pear   la poire

pencil   le crayon

pet   l'animal domestique (m)

some pets

des **animaux** domestiques

peas   les petits pois (m)

penguin   le manchot

piano   le piano

picnic   le pique-nique

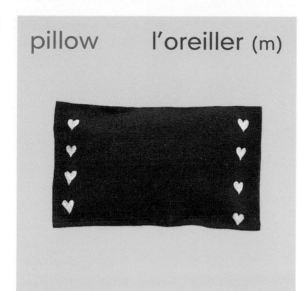

pillow   l'oreiller (m)

plane   l'avion (m)

picture   l'image (f)

pirate   le pirate

These children are dressed as pirates.

Ces enfants sont déguisés en pirates.

plant   la plante

plant   la plante

piece   le morceau, les morceaux

a piece of cake

un morceau de gâteau

pizza   la pizza

plate   l'assiette (f)

There's food on this plate.

Il y a de la nourriture dans cette assiette.

p

play   jouer

They are playing together.

Ils **jouent** ensemble.

pocket   la poche

The boy is putting his hands in his pockets.

Le garçon met ses mains dans ses **poches**.

present   le cadeau, les cadeaux

lots of presents

beaucoup de **cadeaux**

playground   la cour de récréation, l'aire de jeux (f)

police officer   le policier, le gendarme

pretty   joli

These flowers are pretty.

Ces fleurs sont **jolies**.

plum   la prune

potato   la pomme de terre

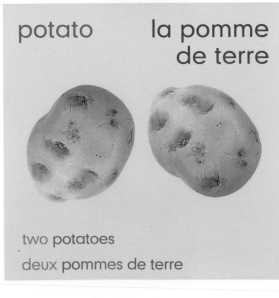

two **potatoes**

deux **pommes de terre**

princess   la princesse

P
Q

prize   **le prix**

The **prize** is a silver cup.

Le **prix** est une coupe en argent.

puppy   **le chiot**

Qq

pull   **tirer**

The boy **pulls** the donkey.

Le garçon **tire** l'âne.

push   **pousser**

This girl is pushing her doll in a pushchair.

Cette fille **pousse** sa poupée dans une poussette.

queen   **la reine**

p

q

puppet   **la marionnette**

put (down)   **poser**

She **puts** the baby **down**.

Elle **pose** le bébé.

quiet   **silencieux (m), silencieuse (f)**

The baby is **quiet**.

Le bébé est **silencieux**.

Rr

rain — **la pluie**

rat — **le rat**

rabbit — **le lapin**

rainbow — **l'arc-en-ciel** (m)

read — **lire**

Tia enjoys **reading**.   Tia aime **lire**.

radio — **la radio**

raspberry — **la framboise**

some raspberries   des framboises

remember — **se rappeler**

A list helps you **remember** what to buy.

Une liste, ça aide à **se rappeler** ce qu'il faut acheter.

rice	le riz

river	la rivière

A river runs through the town.

Une **rivière** traverse la ville.

rocket	la fusée

ride	monter à cheval

Emily likes riding.

Emily aime monter à cheval.

road	la route

They are crossing the **road**.

Ils traversent la **route**.

roof	le toit

a red **roof**   un **toit** rouge

ring	la bague

three rings   trois bagues

robot	le robot

room	la pièce

This house has seven **rooms**.

Cette maison a sept **pièces**.

rope la corde

Ss

sandwich le sandwich

round **rond**

a **round** ball un ballon **rond**

sad **triste**

This little boy looks **sad**.

Ce petit garçon a l'air **triste**.

say **dire**

This woman **says** she's lost her dog.

Cette femme **dit** qu'elle a perdu son chien.

run **courir**

The dogs **run** fast.

Les chiens **courent** vite.

sand **le sable**

They are playing in the **sand**.

Ils jouent sur le **sable**.

scarf **l'écharpe** (f)

school   l'école (f)

secret   le secret

Emily tells Lucy a **secret**.

Emily dit un **secret** à Lucy.

share   partager

They are sharing some fruit.

Elles **partagent** des fruits.

scissors

les ciseaux (m)

see   voir

The firefighter **sees** a dog.

Le pompier **voit** un chien.

sheep   le mouton

sea   la mer

sell   vendre

She **sells** fruit.

Elle **vend** des fruits.

ship   le navire

r
s

shoes **les chaussures** (f)

show **montrer**

Polly **shows** her dad her toy.

Polly **montre** son jouet à son papa.

sister **la sœur**

two **sisters** deux **sœurs**

short **court**

This girl has **short** hair.

Cette fille a les cheveux **courts**.

silver **l'argent** (m)

a **silver** necklace

un collier en **argent**

sit **être assis**

They **are sitting**. Ils **sont assis**.

shout **crier**

Tom and Luke are **shouting**.

FIDO ! FIDO !

Tom et Luke **crient**.

sing **chanter**

Annie loves **singing**.

Annie aime **chanter**.

skin **la peau**

This boy's **skin** is pink.

La peau de ce garçon est rose.

skirt **la jupe**

slow **lent**

Tortoises are very **slow**.   Les tortues sont très lentes.

smile **sourire**

They are smiling.

Ils sourient.

sky **le ciel**

Planes fly in the **sky**.

Les avions volent dans le ciel.

small **petit**

The green fish is small.   Le poisson vert est petit.

snail **l'escargot** (m)

sleep **dormir**

He wants to sleep.

Il veut **dormir**.

smell **sentir**

The cat can **smell** the fish.

Le chat **sent** le poisson.

snake **le serpent**

S

snow   **la neige**

sofa   **le canapé**

These cats are sitting on the **sofa**.

Ces chats sont assis sur le canapé.

spider   **l'araignée** (f)

so   **tellement**

She is **so** surprised.

Elle est **tellement** surprise.

soft   **doux** (m), **douce** (f)

a **soft** blanket

une couverture douce

spoon   **la cuillère**

soap   **le savon**

some   **du** (m), **de la** (f), **des** (plural)

some bread
some flour
some eggs

du pain
de la farine
des œufs

stand   **être debout**

These people **are** all standing.

Ces personnes sont toutes **debout**.

star   l'étoile (f)

shiny stars
des étoiles brillantes

story   l'histoire (f)

a story about firefighters

une histoire sur les pompiers

sun   le soleil

start   commencer

The party starts at 3 o'clock.

La fête commence à trois heures.

strawberry   la fraise

supermarket le supermarché

stop   s'arrêter

Cars have to stop here.

Les voitures doivent s'arrêter ici.

street   la rue

swim   nager

This boy loves swimming.
Ce garçon aime nager.

S

Tt

take — prendre

He takes the box.

Il prend la boîte.

teacher — l'instituteur (m), l'institutrice (f)

table — la table

talk — parler

They **are talking** together.

Elles **parlent** ensemble.

teddy bear — le nounours

tail — la queue

The dog is wagging his **tail**.

Le chien remue sa **queue**.

tall — grand

Emily is **tall** for her age.

Emily est **grande** pour son âge.

teeth — les dents (f)

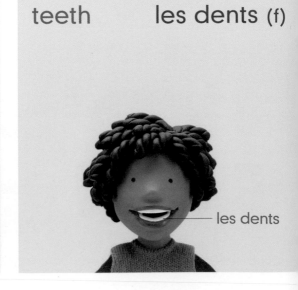

— les dents

T

telephone
le téléphone

He is on the telephone.

Il est au téléphone.

throw   lancer

He is throwing a snowball.

Il lance une boule de neige.

time   l'heure (f)

What time is it?

Quelle heure est-il ?

television
la télévision

thumb   le pouce

le pouce

tired   fatigué

He is
very tired.

Il est très fatigué.

thing   la chose

There are lots of things
on the table.

Il y a beaucoup de choses
sur la table.

tiger   le tigre

toe   l'orteil (m)

l'orteil

t

tomato   **la tomate**

town   **la ville**

train   **le train**

tongue   **la langue**

la langue

toy   **le jouet**

tree   **l'arbre** (m)

towel   **la serviette**

tractor   **le tracteur**

truck   **le camion**

T U V

U u

V v

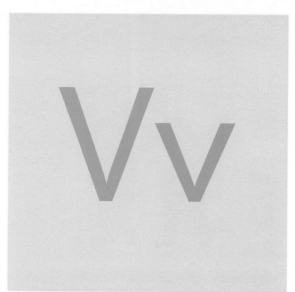

very   **très**

Firefighters are **very** brave.

Les pompiers sont **très** courageux.

---

ugly   **laid**

This fish is **ugly**.

Ce poisson est **laid**.

vase   **le vase**

a **vase** of flowers

un **vase** de fleurs

visit   **visiter**

A clown **is visiting** Paul's house.

Un clown **visite** la maison de Paul.

---

umbrella   **le parapluie**

vegetables   **les légumes (m)**

voice   **la voix**

Ww

walk — marcher

The boy walks with his mum.

Le garçon marche avec sa maman.

warm — chaud

warm clothes

des vêtements chauds

wait — attendre

They are all waiting.

Ils attendent tous.

wall — le mur

They are building a wall.

Ils construisent un mur.

wash — se laver

He is washing himself.

Il se lave.

wake up — se réveiller

It's time to wake up!

Il est l'heure de se réveiller !

want — vouloir

The puppy wants to play.

Le chiot veut jouer.

watch — la montre

W

water   **l'eau** (f)

wet   **mouillé**

This man is all wet!

Cet homme est tout **mouillé** !

whisper   **chuchoter**

The boy is whispering.

Le garçon chuchote.

wave   **saluer**

They **are waving** to their friends.

Ils **saluent** leurs amis.

whale   **la baleine**

win   **gagner**

Who is winning?

Qui gagne ?

wear   **porter**

Chefs wear hats.

Les chefs cuisiniers **portent** des chapeaux.

wheel   **la roue**

window   **la fenêtre**

w

wing   l'aile (f)

This insect has big wings.

Cet insecte a de grandes ailes.

work   travailler

They **work** in a restaurant.

Ils **travaillent** dans un restaurant.

Xx

with   avec

Amy is **with** her mum.

Amy est **avec** sa maman.

worm   le ver de terre

x-ray   la radio

woman   la femme

write   écrire

She is **writing** her name.

Elle **écrit** son nom.

xylophone
le xylophone

W
X
Y
Z

Yy

yet   **encore**

This baby can't walk **yet**.

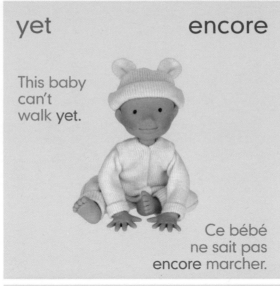

Ce bébé ne sait pas encore marcher.

Zz

yawn   **bâiller**

He is yawning.

Il bâille.

yogurt   **le yaourt**

zebra   **le zèbre**

year   **l'année** (f), **l'an** (m)

This girl is seven **years** old.

Cette fille a sept **ans**.

young   **jeune**

A foal is a **young** horse.

Un poulain est un **jeune** cheval.

zip   **la fermeture éclair**

W

X

Y

Z

Where are they?

Où sont-ils ?

These two pages show some words you use when you want to say where someone or something is.

---

behind — derrière

Andrew is behind Lola.

Andrew est derrière Lola.

---

in — dans

in the drawer — dans le tiroir

---

above — au-dessus de

The plane flies above the clouds.

L'avion vole au-dessus des nuages.

---

between — entre

Sam is between two grown-ups.

Sam est entre deux grandes personnes.

---

in front of — devant

The cars are in front of the house.

Les voitures sont devant la maison.

---

around — autour de

They are sitting around the table.

Ils sont assis autour de la table.

---

here/there — ici/là-bas

I'm here, he's over there.

Je suis ici, il est là-bas.

---

inside — dedans, à l'intérieur

There are people inside.

Il y a des gens à l'intérieur.

into   dans

Ann puts the duckling **into** the pond.

Ann met le poussin **dans** la mare.

opposite   en face de

Tom is sitting **opposite** Leah.

Tom est assis **en face de** Leah.

to/from   à/de

Anna goes **from** her house **to** school by bus.

Anna va **de** sa maison **à** l'école en bus.

next to   à côté de

Patch is sitting **next to** Ted.

Patch est assis **à côté de** Ted.

outside   dehors

These people are **outside**.

Ces personnes sont **dehors**.

under   sous

under the table   **sous** la table

on   sur

The girl is lying **on** the doctor's table.

La fille est allongée **sur** la table du médecin.

over   au-dessus de

The lamb jumps **over** the flowers.

L'agneau saute **au-dessus des** fleurs.

up/down

en haut/en bas

One girl goes **up** when the other is **down**.

Une fille va **en haut** quand l'autre est **en bas**.

I, you, he, she
Je, tu, il, elle

This page shows some words you use when you want to talk about yourself, other people or things.

he   **il**

He has a sister.   Il a une sœur.

we   **nous**

We each have a bag.

Nous avons chacune un sac.

I   **je, j'**

I have a brother.   J'ai un frère.

she   **elle**

She has a doll.   Elle a une poupée.

you   **vous**

Are you all sitting?

Êtes-vous tous assis ?

you   **tu**

Do you know the answer?

Est-ce que tu connais la réponse ?

it   **il** (m), **elle** (f)

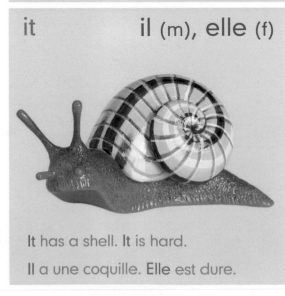

It has a shell. It is hard.

Il a une coquille. Elle est dure.

they   **ils** (m), **elles** (f)

They have lots of dogs.
They are all very cute.

Elles ont beaucoup de chiens.
Ils sont tous très mignons.

Questions
Les questions

This page shows some of the words you can use when you want to ask a question about something.

what   qu'est-ce que

What are you reading?

Qu'est-ce que tu lis ?

which   quel (m), quelle (f)

Which dog do you like best?

Quel chien préfères-tu ?

how   comment

How do you make a cake?

Comment fais-tu un gâteau ?

when   quand

When does the bus arrive?

Quand arrive le bus ?

who   qui

Who is singing?   Qui chante ?

how many   combien

How many shells are there?

Il y a combien de coquillages ?

where   où

Where are my friends?

Où sont mes amis ?

why   pourquoi

Why is Laura sad?

Pourquoi est-ce que Laura est triste ?

Colours   Les couleurs (f)

white
blanc (m),
blanche (f)

blue
bleu (m), bleue (f)

pink
rose

green
vert (m),
verte (f)

orange
orange

yellow
jaune

red
rouge

grey
gris (m), grise (f)

purple
violet (m),
violette (f)

black
noir (m),
noire (f)

brown
marron

Shapes   Les formes (f)

circle
le cercle

oval
l'ovale (m)

heart
le cœur

rectangle
le rectangle

star
l'étoile (f)

triangle
le triangle

crescent
le croissant

square
le carré

Numbers   Les nombres (m)

one	un
two	deux
three	trois
four	quatre
five	cinq
six	six
seven	sept
eight	huit
nine	neuf
ten	dix

Months
Les mois (m)

January	janvier
February	février
March	mars
April	avril
May	mai
June	juin
July	juillet
August	août
September	septembre
October	octobre
November	novembre
December	décembre

Days
Les jours (m)

Monday	lundi
Tuesday	mardi
Wednesday	mercredi
Thursday	jeudi
Friday	vendredi
Saturday	samedi
Sunday	dimanche

Seasons
Les saisons (f)

spring	le printemps
summer	l'été (m)
autumn	l'automne (m)
winter	l'hiver (m)

Using your dictionary

When you have looked up a word, here are some things you can find out.

drink   la boisson

a cold **drink**   une **boisson** fraîche

You can see the French translation of the word.

You can see a picture of the word, or a way of using the word.

pillow	l'oreiller (m)

The letter m in brackets tells you that the word is masculine.

bee	l'abeille (f)

The letter f in brackets tells you that the word is feminine.

Masculine or feminine?

In French, all nouns, or "naming" words such as "boy" and "house", are either masculine or feminine. The French word for "the" is <u>le</u> for masculine nouns and <u>la</u> for feminine words. The French word for "a" or "an" is <u>un</u> for masculine nouns and <u>une</u> for feminine nouns.

Sometimes you can guess whether a noun is feminine or masculine – for example, "boy" is masculine (le garçon). Other times, you need to check the dictionary.

If a noun begins with a, e, i, o, or u, and sometimes h, then le or la is shortened to <u>l'</u>.

Plurals

"Plural" means "more than one". The French for "the" when you are talking about more than one is <u>les</u>, for both masculine and feminine nouns. You also add <u>s</u> at the end of the noun, as you do in English:

boy	le garçon
boys	les garçons

If the noun ends in s already, you don't need to add another s:

mouse	la souris
mice	les souris

A few nouns have a different spelling in the plural.

horse	le cheval, les chevaux

Nouns with a different plural are shown like this.

Adjectives

"Describing" words, such as "small", "cold" or "happy", are adjectives.

In English, an adjective is always spelled the same, whatever it is describing. In French, the endings of an adjective change, depending on whether the noun is feminine or masculine, singular or plural.

For example, the French word for "hot" is "chaud":

a hot bath   un bain chaud

For a feminine noun, you add <u>e</u> to the end of the adjective (unless it ends in e already):

hot water   l'eau chaude

For masculine plurals, you add <u>s</u> to the end of the adjective (unless it ends in s or x already):

hot dishes   les plats chauds

For feminine plurals, you add <u>es</u>:

hot drinks   les boissons chaudes

A few adjectives have slightly different feminine forms. They are shown in the dictionary like this:

good   bon (m), bonne (f)
long   long (m), longue (f)

A very few adjectives also have a different form before masculine nouns beginning with a, e, i, o, u, and sometimes h. They are shown like this:

old   vieux (m), vieil (m), vieille (f)
an old cat   un vieux chat
an old donkey   un vieil âne
an old woman   une vieille femme

In English, adjectives usually go before the noun they are describing. In French, most adjectives go after the noun:

a blue flower   une fleur bleue
a soft blanket   une couverture douce

A few very common adjectives go before the noun they are describing:

a good book   un bon livre
a big garden   un grand jardin
a fat cat   un gros chat
a young child   un jeune enfant
a pretty flower   une jolie fleur
a long dress   une longue robe
a bad smell   une mauvaise odeur
a small boy   un petit garçon
an old house   une vieille maison
a naughty dog   un vilain chien

Verbs

"Doing" words, such as "walk" or "laugh", are called verbs. In English, verbs don't change very much, whoever is doing them:

I walk

you walk

he walks

she walks

we walk

you walk

they walk

In French, the endings change much more. Many verbs work in a similar way to the one below. The verb is in the present – the form you use to talk about what's happening now.

to give	donner
I give	je donne
you give*	tu donnes
he gives	il donne
she gives	elle donne
we give	nous donnons
you give*	vous donnez
they give	ils donnent
	elles donnent

When you look up a verb in the dictionary, you will find the "to" form, together with a sentence or phrase that shows how the verb can be used. All these sentences use the verb in the present form.

Two useful verbs

Two of the most useful verbs to know are "to be" and "to have". Here they are in French, in the present form:

to be	être
I am	je suis
you are*	tu es
he is	il est
she is	elle est
we are	nous sommes
you are*	vous êtes
they are	ils sont
	elles sont

to have	avoir
I have	j'ai
you have*	tu as
he has	il a
she has	elle a
we have	nous avons
you have*	vous avez
they have	ils ont
	elles ont

Mostly, you use them in just the same way as you do in English:

I have a sister.	J'ai une sœur.
She is tall.	Elle est grande.

Just sometimes, it isn't the verb you expect:

I am eight.	J'ai huit ans.

* In French, you use "tu" for one person, either a young person or someone you know well. You use "vous" for more than one person, or for an older person or someone you don't know very well.

French word list

à	at, to	l'année (f)	year
à côté de	next to	l'anniversaire (m)	birthday
à l'intérieur	inside	août	August
l'abeille (f)	bee	après	after
acheter	to buy	l'après-midi (m)	afternoon
l'agneau (m)	lamb	l'araignée (f)	spider
aider	to help	l'arbre (m)	tree
l'aigle (m)	eagle	l'arc-en-ciel (m)	rainbow
l'aiguille (f)	needle	l'argent (m)	money, silver
l'aile (f)	wing	s'arrêter	to stop
aimer	to like, to love	l'assiette (f)	plate
l'air (m), les airs (m)	air	l'astronaute (m/f)	astronaut
l'aire de jeux (f)	playground	attendre	to wait
aller	to go	attraper	to catch
l'alphabet (m)	alphabet	au-dessus de	above, over
l'ambulance (f)	ambulance	l'autobus (m)	bus
l'ami (m), l'amie (f)	friend	l'automne (m)	autumn
l'an (m)	year	autour de	around
l'âne (m)	donkey	l'autre (m/f)	other
l'ange (m)	angel	avec	with
l'animal (m)	animal	l'avion (m)	plane
l'animal domestique (m)	pet	avoir besoin	to need

French	English	French	English
avril	April	la boue	mud
la bague	ring	le bout	end
bâiller	to yawn	le bouton	button
le bain	bath	le bras	arm
le baiser	kiss	la brosse	brush
la baleine	whale	le bruit	noise
la balle	ball	le bus	bus
le ballon	ball	la cacahuète	peanut
la banane	banana	se cacher	to hide
la barrière	gate	le cadeau	present
le bateau	boat	le camion	truck
beaucoup	a lot, lots	le canapé	sofa
le bébé	baby	le canard	duck
la bicyclette	bicycle	la capuche	hood
les bijoux (m)	jewellery	la carotte	carrot
blanc (m), blanche (f)	white	le carré	square
bleu	blue	la carte	map, card
la boisson	drink	la ceinture	belt
la boîte	box	le cercle	circle
le bol	bowl	le cerf-volant	kite
bon (m), bonne (f)	good	la cerise	cherry
les bottes (f)	boots	la chaise	chair
la bouche	mouth	le champignon	mushroom
la bouchée	bite	chanter	to sing

le chapeau	hat	la coccinelle	ladybird
chaque	each	le cochon d'Inde	guinea pig
le chat	cat	le cœur	heart
le château	castle	le collier	necklace
le chaton	kitten	combien	how many, how much
chaud	warm, hot	commencer	to start
les chaussures (f)	shoes	comment	how
le cheval	horse	conduire	to drive
les cheveux (m)	hair	construire	to build
la cheville	ankle	la corde	rope
la chèvre	goat	le cou	neck
le chien	dog	le coude	elbow
le chiffre	number	la couleur	colour
le chiot	puppy	la cour de récréation	playground
le chocolat	chocolate	courir	to run
la chose	thing	court	short
chuchoter	to whisper	le couteau	knife
le ciel	sky	la couverture	blanket
cinq	five	le crayon	pencil
les ciseaux (m)	scissors	creuser	to dig
le citron	lemon	crier	to shout
clair	light	le croissant	crescent
la clé	key	la cuillère	spoon
la clef	key	la cuisine	kitchen

dans	in, into	le doigt	finger
danser	to dance	donner	to give
de	of, from	donner un coup de pied	to kick
de la (f)	any, some	dormir	to sleep
décembre	December	doux (m), douce (f)	soft
dedans	inside	le dragon	dragon
dehors	outside	le drapeau	flag
le déjeuner	lunch	du (m)	any, some
demander	to ask	dur	hard
démanger	to itch	l'eau (f)	water
le/la dentiste	dentist	l'écharpe (f)	scarf
les dents (f)	teeth	l'école (f)	school
déplacer	to move	écouter	to listen
derrière	behind	écrire	to write
des (plural)	any, some	l'éléphant (m)	elephant
le désordre	mess	elle	she, it
dessiner	to draw	elles	they (f)
deux	two	embrasser	to hug
devant	in front of	l'emploi (m)	work, job
dimanche	Sunday	en bas	down
le dinosaure	dinosaur	en face de	opposite
dire	to say	en haut	up
dix	ten	encore	again, yet, another
le docteur	doctor	l'encre (f)	ink

endormi	asleep	la fête	party
entendre	to hear	le feu	fire
entre	between	la feuille	leaf
l'escargot (m)	snail	février	February
est	is	le filet	net
l'été (m)	summer	la fille	girl
l'étoile (f)	star	la fleur	flower
être assis	to sit	la forêt	forest
être couché	to lie	les formes (f)	shapes
être debout	to stand	fort	loud, strong
éveillé	awake	la fourchette	fork
fâché	angry	la fourmi	ant
faire	to do, to make	la fraise	strawberry
faire la cuisine	to cook	la framboise	raspberry
faire mal	to hurt	frapper	to hit
la famille	family	le frère	brother
le fantôme	ghost	froid	cold
fatigué	tired	le fromage	cheese
la fée	fairy	les fruits (m)	fruit
la femme	woman	la fusée	rocket
la fenêtre	window	gagner	to win
le fer à repasser	iron	les gants (m)	gloves
la ferme	farm	le garçon	boy
la fermeture éclair	zip	le gâteau	cake

le géant	giant	huit	eight
le gendarme	police officer	ici	here
le genou	knee	l'idée (f)	idea
les gens (m/f)	people	il	he, it
la girafe	giraffe	l'île (f)	island
la glace	ice, ice cream, mirror	ils	they (m)
grand	big, tall	l'image (f)	picture
la grande personne	grown-up	l'infirmier (m), l'infirmière (f)	nurse
la grenouille	frog	l'insecte (m)	insect
gris	grey	l'instituteur (m), l'institutrice (f)	teacher
gros (m), grosse (f)	fat	l'invitation (f)	invitation
habiter	to live	jamais	never
le hamster	hamster	la jambe	leg
l'hélicoptère (m)	helicopter	janvier	January
l'herbe (f)	grass	le jardin	garden
l'heure (f)	time, o'clock	jaune	yellow
heureux (m), heureuse (f)	happy	je, j'	I
le hibou	owl	le jean, les jeans	jeans
hier	yesterday	le jeu	game
l'histoire (f)	story	jeudi	Thursday
l'hiver (m)	winter	jeune	young
l'homme (m)	man	joli	pretty
l'hôpital (m)	hospital	jongler	to juggle
l'huile (f)	oil	jouer	to play

le jouet	toy	lire	to read
le jour	day	le lit	bed
le journal	newspaper	le livre	book
juillet	July	long (m), longue (f)	long
juin	June	lundi	Monday
la jungle	jungle	la lune	moon
la jupe	skirt	les lunettes (f)	glasses
le jus	juice	la machine	machine
le kangourou	kangaroo	la magie	magic
le ketchup	ketchup	mai	May
là-bas	there	la main	hand
laid	ugly	maintenant	now
laisser	to let	la maison	house, home
le lait	milk	le manchot	penguin
la lampe	lamp	manger	to eat
lancer	to throw	le manteau	coat
la langue	tongue	marcher	to walk
le lapin	rabbit	mardi	Tuesday
se laver	to wash	la marionnette	puppet
les légumes (m)	vegetables	marron	brown
lent	slow	mars	March
la lettre	letter	le matin	morning
les lèvres (f)	lips	mauvais	bad
le lion	lion	le médecin	doctor

la mer	sea	noir	black, dark
mercredi	Wednesday	la noisette	hazelnut
le miel	honey	la noix	walnut
le miroir	mirror	le nom	name
le mois	month	le nombre	number
le monstre	monster	le nounours	teddy bear
la montagne	mountain	la nourriture	food
monter à cheval	to ride (a horse)	nous	we
la montre	watch	novembre	November
montrer	to show	le nuage	cloud
le morceau	piece	la nuit	night
la moto	motorbike	le numéro	number
mouillé	wet	octobre	October
le mouton	sheep	l'œil (m)	eye
le mur	wall	l'œuf (m)	egg
la musique	music	l'oie (f)	goose
nager	to swim	l'oignon (m)	onion
le navire	ship	l'oiseau (m)	bird
ne...pas	not	l'or (m)	gold
la neige	snow	orange	orange (colour)
neuf	nine	l'orange (f)	orange (fruit)
neuf (m), neuve (f)	new	l'ordinateur (m)	computer
le nez	nose	l'oreille (f)	ear
le nid	nest	l'oreiller (m)	pillow

l'orteil (m)	toe	la pendule	clock
l'os (m)	bone	personne	nobody
ou	or	petit	little, small
où	where	le petit déjeuner (m)	breakfast
l'ours (m)	bear	les petits pois (m)	peas
ouvrir	to open	le piano	piano
l'ovale (m)	oval	la pièce	room
la page	page	le pied	foot
le pain	bread	la pierre précieuse	jewel
le palais	palace	la pieuvre	octopus
le panda	panda	le pique-nique	picnic
le panier	basket	le pirate	pirate
le papier	paper	la pizza	pizza
le papillon	butterfly	la plage	beach
le parapluie	umbrella	la plante	plant
le parc	park	pleurer	to cry
parler	to talk	la pluie	rain
partager	to share	plus	more
les pâtes (f)	pasta	la poche	pocket
la peau	skin	la poire	pear
la pêche	peach	le poisson	fish
peindre	to paint	le poisson rouge	goldfish
la pelleteuse	digger	le policier	police officer
la pelouse	grass	la pomme	apple

la pomme de terre	potato	la question	question
le pompier	firefighter	la queue	tail, queue
la porte	door	qui	who
porter	to wear, to carry	la radio	radio, x-ray
poser	to put (down)	le raisin	grapes
le pot	jar	se rappeler	to remember
le pouce	thumb	le rat	rat
le poulet	chicken	le rectangle	rectangle
la poupée	doll	regarder	to look (at)
pourquoi	why	la reine	queen
pousser	to push, to grow	le renard	fox
pouvoir	can, to be able to	réveillé	awake
prendre	to take	se réveiller	to wake up
près	near	rien	nothing
la princesse	princess	rire	to laugh
le printemps	spring	la rivière	river
le prix	prize, price	le riz	rice
profond	deep	la robe	dress
la prune	plum	le robot	robot
le puzzle	jigsaw puzzle	le roi	king
quand	when	rond	round
quatre	four	rose	pink
quel (m), quelle (f)	which	la roue	wheel
qu'est-ce que	what	rouge	red

la route	road	six	six
la rue	street	la sœur	sister
le sable	sand	le sol	floor
le sac	bag	le soleil	sun
la saison	season	sont	are
sale	dirty	sourire	to smile
saluer	to wave	la souris	mouse
samedi	Saturday	sous	under
le sandwich	sandwich	souvent	often
sauter	to jump	le stylo	pen
sauter à cloche-pied	to hop	le supermarché	supermarket
le savon	soap	sur	on, about
sec (m), sèche (f)	dry	la table	table
le secret	secret	le tambour	drum
sentir	to smell, to feel	la tasse	cup
sept	seven	le téléphone	telephone
septembre	September	la télévision	television
le serpent	snake	tellement	so
la serviette	towel	la Terre	Earth
seulement	only	la terre	ground
si	if	la tête	head
silencieux (m), silencieuse (f)	quiet	le tigre	tiger
le singe	monkey	tirer	to pull
la sirène	mermaid	le toit	roof

la tomate	tomato	les vêtements (m)	clothes
toujours	always	vide	empty
tout (m) (tous), toute (f) (toutes)	all	vieux (m), vieil (m), vieille (f)	old
le tracteur	tractor	vilain	naughty, ugly
le train	train	la ville	town
travailler	to work	violet (m), violette (f)	purple
très	very	le visage	face
le triangle	triangle	visiter	to visit
triste	sad	vite	fast
trois	three	voir	to see
le trou	hole	le voisin	neighbour
tu	you	la voiture	car
un (m), une (f)	a, an, one	la voiture de pompiers	fire engine
une fois	once	la voix	voice
la vache	cow	voler	to fly, to steal
le vase	vase	vouloir	to want
le vélo	bicycle	vous	you
vendre	to sell	le xylophone	xylophone
vendredi	Friday	le yaourt	yogurt
venir	to come	le zèbre	zebra
le ver de terre	worm		
le verre	glass		
vert	green		
la veste	jacket		

Hear the words on the internet

If you can use the internet and your computer can play sounds, you can listen to all the French words in this dictionary, read by a French person.

Go to the Usborne Quicklinks Website at www.usborne-quicklinks.com Type in the keywords **very first dictionary in french** and follow the simple instructions. Try listening to the words and then saying them yourself. This will help you learn to speak French easily and well. Always follow the safety rules on the right when you are using the internet.

What you need

To play the French words, your computer may need a small program called a media player, such as RealPlayer® or Windows® Media Player. These programs are free, and if you don't already have one, you can download a copy from www.usborne-quicklinks.com

Internet safety rules

Ask your parent's or guardian's permission before you connect to the internet and make sure you follow these simple rules:

• Never give out information about yourself, such as your real name, address, phone number or the name of your school.

• If a site asks you to log in or register by typing your name or email address, ask permission from an adult first.

Notes for parents or guardians

The Very First Dictionary area of the Usborne Quicklinks Website contains no links to external websites. However, other areas of Usborne Quicklinks do contain links to websites that do not belong to Usborne Publishing. The links are regularly reviewed and updated, but Usborne Publishing is not responsible, and does not accept liability, for the content or availability of any website other than its own, or for any exposure to harmful, offensive or inaccurate material which may appear on the Web.

We recommend that children are supervised while on the internet, that they do not use internet chat rooms and that you use internet filtering software to block unsuitable material. Please ensure that your children follow the safety guidelines above.

For more information, see the "Net Help" area of the Usborne Quicklinks Website at www.usborne-quicklinks.com

French language consultant: Lorraine Beurton-Sharp

Edited by Fiona Chandler

Additional design by Stephanie Jones

Photography by Howard Allman & MMStudios

With thanks to Paul Allen, Ben Denne and Sam Taplin, and to Staedtler UK for providing the Fimo® material for models. Vehicles supplied by Bruder® Toys.

First published in 2008 by Usborne Publishing Ltd., Usborne House, 83-85 Saffron Hill, London EC1N 8RT, England.
Copyright ©2008 Usborne Publishing Ltd.